The Infinite Knot
Josephine Abbott

smith|doorstop

Published 2017 by
smith|doorstop books
The Poetry Business
Bank Street Arts
32–40 Bank Street
Sheffield S1 2DS

Copyright © Josephine Abbott 2017
All Rights Reserved

ISBN 978-1-910367-81-0
Typeset by Utter
Printed by People for Print, Sheffield

smith|doorstop books are a member of Inpress:
www.inpressbooks.co.uk.

Distributed by NBN International, Airport Business Centre,
10 Thornbury Road Plymouth PL6 7PP

The Poetry Business gratefully acknowledges the support of
Arts Council England.

Contents

- (i) CONSOLATION 5
- (ii) SISTER 6
- (iii) A SURE CHEMISTRY 7
- (iv) ZERO DECIBELS 8
- (v) WHITE NOISE 9
- (vi) CELTIC TREE ALPHABET 10
- (vii) FALLING FOSS, NORTH YORKSHIRE 11
- (viii) BORROWED SCENERY 12
- (ix) THE MOON HAS BURST ITS BANKS 13
- (x) TRYING NOT TO THINK 14
- (xi) A PAIR OF SWALLOWS 15
- (x) CHINESE PAINTING 17
- (ix) TWO SWANS ON THE DERWENT, DERBYSHIRE 18
- (viii) THE PHILEMON & BAUCIS SYNDROME 19
- (vii) THE INEXACTNESS OF RAIN 22
- (vi) NOCTURNE 23
- (v) ALCHEMY 24
- (iv) WHEN 25
- (iii) A CHEMICAL FORMULA FOR FIRE 26
- (ii) BEES 27
- (i) THE RAIN GHOSTS 28

For DJA, for all the years

(i)

Light years from here, on Luhman 16B
it's pouring down drops of iron
from metal clouds. Billions of miles away

there's a planet (HD189733B)
where it rains molten glass
blown sideways by 4,000 mph winds.

This rain that prickles my skin awake
and puts my heart to sleep
is nothing to the lightning storm on Saturn

that blasts methane to carbon,
compresses it, hardens it, drops it
as chunks of diamond.

It's only a bit of rain. I won't melt.
It's not that cruel to bury someone in it.

(ii)

Click <u>sister</u> and my memory opens:
in the living-room, ribbons of sun

are stirred by flecks of dust.
No ordinary dust, this, but

atoms and molecules of her soul
I can try to gather and reassemble.

Click <u>here</u> and I can hear
all our voices, childish and new –

still with this early morning in them
and arguing about next-to-nothing –

after that one sentence
change to old.

All that time ago, and still,
whenever there's dust like that –

restless in a window of early sun –
I click <u>sister</u> and my memory opens.

(iii)

> *The world has a sure chemistry, by which it*
> *extracts what is excellent in its children*
> — R.W. Emerson

So after all, I'm a set of chemicals
in my own alembic, cucurbit, retort,
being heated and distilled.

There's someone who watches and measures,
who weighs and analyses how well-filtered,
how separated, how sublimated I am.

But what will be extracted
is anyone's guess. No spreadsheet,
no number of chemical equations,

can predict when something will vaporise,
combust, or be lost in pieces of broken glass.
I'm being stirred over a Bunsen Burner

by an alchemist with a recipe, hoping
to turn any little part of me to gold.

(iv)

It was when we braved the silence,
the unmapped, dangerous silence,

and found the kind of exhilaration
that comes from risk – exhilaration

like freefall in a clear sky – and stripped
ourselves of everything but the stripped-

to-the-core quietness of here, now, daring
to lose ourselves in stillness, daring

not to need to speak, that we started hearing
things below the threshold of hearing –

a pulse, a breath, the open air
of a wide-open future, the bare air

of words not mattering – and learned to love
the unhearable, the helpless bits of love.

(v)

all I remember about white noise
is nothing to do with the science –

the frequencies, waves,
sound pressure levels –

nothing to do with amplitudes
or sound intensities

or the analogy
with white light,

nothing about recording it
or randomly generating it;

just the modulation of your voice
when you told me

how it always sounds
like rain, or the sea in a shell

(vi)

There's a tree-alphabet –
the *beth-luis-nion* –
I want to learn;

it stamps messages on the sky
using angles of twigs and branch,
branch and trunk;

uses the line and slant
of central stems and veins
to write its code on leaves.

I'll practise every day
some words in holly, hazel and willow,
some phrases of oak, ivy, birch, ash,

until the stark lines of the language
at last make some kind of sense.

(vii)

These threads of water crashing on stone
are shouting something important;

this spun silk against rock
resonates through my bones.

Here's one way the earth measures time:
it dissolves itself grain by grain,

molecule by molecule. By comparison,
my small life is beside the point.

The water I've just seen has already gone,
taking with it some of the ground

I'm standing on. And there's something sad
in the way I still can't understand

what this fraying of water and land
wants to tell me in a thousand different voices.

(viii)

I'll have to give the mountains back,
and that blueness there, in the distance,

that trail of mist, will be all that's left.
The sea's the exact colour, by sheer coincidence,

of concrete and road, and so is invisible.
When I borrow wind and rain,

I'll hang one of them for hours in the silver birch;
leave the other on the grass like polished grain.

> Today, the clouds I've taken have changed
> from cotton wool to old cotton sheet
>
> pegged out over the garden. Tonight
> I'm going to have a clear sky, complete
>
> with a full moon just within reach:
> an irresistible, halved white peach.

(ix)

The moon has burst its banks
and the bedroom's flooded.

Things are lost underwater;
are dead, white, floating.

The bedding's drenched with silver
and the light that laps at the pillows,
chrome-plates your face and shoulder.

Against the window,
the shadow of the birch
is propped like a ladder.

The moon's as wide awake as I am:
brimming with glad-to-be-alive.

(x)

I'm not listening to the clock; it's my breathing
that counts out the time. I try not to think

that the buzz of the computer, the hum of water
is how blood runs through my veins. I hear you

upstairs. Ten thousand images in your walk.
This rain sounds like the crackle of fire.

I'm supposed to find an inner fire,
but all I do is listen to you walk.

Running through me like a core, is you:
not fire or electricity, but water.

Time's passing. I try not to think
about that. All that matters is the breathing.

(xi)

Just when we needed it most
        we saw them: side by side,
waiting for us to notice them,
        balanced certainly on the wire,
to show us how it's done –
        like this, like this. We, though,
were heavy-boned and lost.

        How far had they come?
All that counted was that we were here
        and that side by side we could watch
their black ribbon tailfeathers
        pinned against the sky:
mourning in early summer.
        What changed us was their flight:

they fell together, synchronised,
        sure of never falling,
and took us with them. Air breathed
        through the tips of our fingers
and through the down under our wings;
        it was like flesh to lean against
and stopped us from saying anything.

    Solid ground turned to solid sky;
the earth was unfathomable below us.
    Our eyes saw differently now;
our hearts weighed next to nothing
    and our bones were hollow as pipes.
A pair of swallows in flight
    and loss held in the balance.

(x)

When mist spills in over the moors –
ink-and-wash over silk – it changes us.

We hadn't seen it coming, and now
disoriented, dissolving, touched on the raw,

we're timeless, out of place and afraid.
All we have is the insubstantial road

that blurs under our feet; we're being dabbed away
and transformed into an oriental painting of sky.

Minutes ago, the moor was all horizon:
flat, round as a sundial, and with us as gnomon;

now it's Big-Cloud-brushed and beautiful
and we're scared, calligraphed to a standstill.

We're being painted into a poem with no sound;
into a landscape with no end of air and water.

(ix)

Under clouds like these,
two swans shed pools of whiteness;

are symmetrical as bedside lamps;
reflect each other exactly, faithfully.

Their stillness is catching:
the water round them is flat, polished;

their air closed like a bedroom door.
Even the rain doesn't seem to reach them,

shut out by sheer brightness.
Every wavelength of light flicks off them;

they shrug off everything except
their need to stare in each other's mirror.

(viii)

Philemon & Baucis:
Ovid, The Metamorphoses, Bk 8, ll 616-724

When the time comes, we'll be ready.
By then, I'll have noticed the roughening

of my skin, and how my limbs are stiffening.
You will be starting to come into leaf,

losing your eyesight, growing deaf.
'Vale, o coniunx'. There are worse things,

I have to say, than having annual rings
to be counted by instead of human years,

and only insects and birds – not fears –
to settle down on us every night.

Instead of losing our senses and our height,
there'll be a slow self-grafting as we grow

and touch more closely than skin to skin. Oh,
when the time comes, we'll be more than ready.

∞ ∞ ∞

It's the shard of pottery that gets me:
the detail of how she uses it to wedge
the leg of the wobbly table, casually.
She's done it a hundred times before.

She keeps it on the shelf, handy
in case of visitors. Its pattern
is faded and difficult to see
but fresh as ever in her mind's eye.

This table's always been rickety;
this pot, one she couldn't bear to chuck.
This is her – their – fidelity:
their keeping faith with broken things.

A wonky table, a piece of pottery,
a thousands-of-years-old story.

∞ ∞ ∞

A husband-and-wife tree, they call it:
      side by side, limbs in a tangle,

caught forever not *in flagrante delicto*
      but in growing together.

Their slow grafting has made them
>	monumental, like effigies.

Someone has built a low wall round it;
>	rags hang from the branches;

shreds of paper, cloth, coins and stones
>	are wedged and embedded in it

as if the tree might notice prayers, nod,
>	and hand them up to the sky.

Marriage-tree: double-bedded;
>	deep-rooted; far-eyed.

(vii)

it's the inexactness of rain –
the looseness of the threads
and the washed-out look of it –

that we find as comfortable
as swimming in a flat, lazy sea;
there's a worn-out silk look to it

in our afternoon bedroom
damp-lit with it
that's dull and shadowless

and kinder to the pair of us
than a tarnished mirror

(vi)

We're not scared of darkness. The dark
        is when light is at its most exuberant.

There's no such thing as drowning in the dark
        when we can hang on to shreds of light

the way we cling to each other. In the dead of night,
        a highlight on a shoulder or hip, or in an eye

tantalises like fruit and makes any night sweet.
        Dark grows upward. Light dawdles in the sky

like a lover who has to leave. There's always
        enough light to hear by. We can hear

the sea hundreds of miles away
        and the white noise of electricity.

This is when light is at its best.
        We're not afraid. Not of the dark.

(v)

A scanning electron microscope,
atomic-force, super-resolution,

looks into the nano-dimension;
gives it a focused-ion beam poke

with a thermo-chemical pen.
The nano-architect in the nano-landscape

with endless patience and hocus-pocus
measures, moves, measures again;

reconfigures on a molecular scale
the impossible-to-work-with surface;

shapes and re-shapes the face
of the smallest planet thinkable;

micro-fabricates with a shaky hand
any world we'd like, on a grain of sand.

(iv)

When I am a salamander, I'll
learn to breathe through my skin;

I'll get the knack of regenerating
skin, muscle, bone, a limb, an eye;

I'll dress in flameproof clothes
and dance all day in the fire.

Daughter of fire, elemental,
the pure matter of alchemy,

I'll surprise you all one day
by flaring like a spit of flame

out of a hollow burning log,
a fire-spirit flitting out of death.

I'll be unbreakable
when I'm a salamander.

(iii)

The chemical formula for fire isn't simple:
there's something that burns, and ignition,

then sequence after sequence of reaction.
Not-quite-gas, not-liquid, not-solid,

fire breathes air; stirs itself into it
like red ink into water. It feeds on

and needs the material it destroys;
the heat and light that come out of it

come from the deaths of things.
Each flake of soot and ash, each fleck of dust,

flowers red-gold for a millisecond
in a glory of sublimation.

We're just a couple of flames, you and me,
in a never-that-simple formula for fire.

(ii)

They come with their own soundtrack:
a sustained note on a cello.

They've altered the light somehow; tilted it
to a strange angle, the way snow does

and stirred themselves into the garden
in an unstormy way. Calm. Unrandom.

They hold a note somewhere below middle C
and tighten into a corner, onto a fence-post.

They belong in the sun
but are looking for a dark place,

comers and goers between
overworlds and underworlds;

little servants of the gods; dead souls.
There's something primitive about them:

the way they're singing to themselves,
and me, their Old English name: *ymbe*.

(i)

Rain ghosts are pattering on the glass;
what they want is to be let in.

They have something they're dying to tell you
and only one syllable they can use to whisper it.

We've come – they'll say – out of the soil;
out of the river and sea and clouds;

we're ship and wood and all that's lost at sea
carried and scattered against your window;

we're particles of brick and slate and garden;
molecules of paint and tree and cloth

washed off in a forgotten downpour;
we're skin cells and sweat and everyone's DNA

dissolved and rearranged by rain.
Water remembers everything.